Cactus of the Southwest

Nora and Rick Bowers

Adventure Quick Guides
IDENTIFY CACTI WITH EASE

DEDICATION

Our enduring love for Beth, the best of sisters!

ACKNOWLEDGMENTS

Our enormous gratitude to Matt Johnson, good friend and cactus guru, for his patient tutoring over the years, and also for reviewing photographs and text. Range maps produced by Matt Johnson, digitized by Anthony Hertzel.

RICK AND NORA BOWERS

Nora Mays Bowers is the author of seven books including *Cactus of Arizona Field Guide* and *Cactus of Texas Field Guide*. Rick Bowers, a naturalist who led nature tours for 25 years, has photographs in many field guides including *Wildflowers of Arizona Field Guide* and *Wildflowers of Texas Field Guide*. Nora and Rick wrote the Kaufman Field Guide *Mammals of North America* with Kenn Kaufman.

PHOTO CREDITS

Cover photo: Common Beehive Cactus by Rick and Nora Bowers

John Bregar: 22 (Missouri Foxtail Cactus-both) **Michelle Cloud-Hughes, 2016:** 8 (California Cholla Cactus), 9 (Wolf Cholla Cactus, Gander Cholla Flower, Chuckwalla Cholla-both), 11 (Sagebrush Club Cholla-both, Chaparral Prickly Pear flower), 13 (Coastal Prickly Pear flower), 14 (Pinkava Prickly Pear flower), 16 (Coast Barrel Cactus flower), 21 (Mojave Spinystar-both), 23 (Smallflower Fishhook Cactus flower) 26 (Navajo Pincushion flower) **John Crossley, The American Southwest:** 12 (Rio Grande Prickly Pear cactus) **Mark Dimmitt©Arizona-Sonora Desert Museum:** 11 (Pancake Prickly Pear flower) **Alan English:** 8 (Desert Christmas Cholla cactus) **David J. Ferguson, Albuquerque, New Mexico:** 10 (Devil Club Cholla flower, Club Cholla Cactus), 12 (Rio Grande Prickly Pear flower), 14 (Pinkava Prickly Pear cactus) **Gina Glenne:** 24 (Colorado Hookless Cactus-both) **Greg Goodwin:** 26 (Navajo Pincushion cactus) **Sheri Hagwood:** 25 (Mountain Ball Cactus flower) **Bill Hendricks:** 9 (Thistle Cholla flower) **Matthew B. Johnson:** 14 (Plains Prickly Pear flower), 15 (Emory Barrel flower), 18 (Bonker Hedgehog flower), 20 (Woven-spine Pineapple Cactus-both) **Gertrud Konings, Biologist:** 6 (Barbed Wire Cactus flower), 10 (Icicle Cholla flower), 14 (Potts Prickly Pear flower), 16 (Dahlia Hedgehog flower), 24 (Short-hook Fishhook Cactus flower), 27 (Button Cactus-both) 27 (Ping Pong Ball Cactus flower) **Ries Lindley:** 25 (Greenflower Pincushion flower, Wright Pincushion flower) **©Gary A. Monroe/USDA=NRCS:** 6 (Golden Cereus flower), 8 (Diamond-plated Pencil Cholla flower, Coastal Cholla flower), 9 (Wolf Cholla flower), 14 (Grizzly Bear Prickly Pear flower), 19 (Johnson Pineapple Cactus flower), 22 (Mojave Fishhook Cactus-both) **©Keir Morse:** 9 (Gander Cholla cactus), 19 (Cushion Foxtail Cactus-both) **Jerry Murray, 2016:** 15 (Brittle Prickly Pear flower) **Stan Shebs:** 10 (Parish Club Cholla flower) **J Scott Peterson@plants.usda.gov:** 11 (Chaparral Prickly Pear cactus) **©Gary Dean Regner:** 12 (Chisos Mountain Prickly Pear flower) **Jim Rorabaugh:** 25 (Corkyseed Fishhook Pincushion flower) **Daniela Roth:** 24 (Mesa Verde Fishhook Cactus-both), 26 (Brady Pincushion-both) **Phillip Ruttenbur:** 10 (Schott Club Cholla flower), 14 (Chenille Prickly Pear cactus) **©Al Schneider, www.swcoloradowildflowers.com:** 25 (Mountain Ball Cactus) **Robert Sivinski:** 10 (Club Cholla flower), 23 (Clover Eagle-claw Cactus-both) **Gene Sturla:** 8 (Klein Pencil Cholla flower) **Bill Sullivan:** 15 (Many-headed Barrel flower) **Stan Tekiela:** 6 (Saguaro cactus, Organ Pipe cactus, Jumping Cholla cactus), 13 (Black-spine Prickly Pear cactus), 15 (Emory Barrel cactus) **Dorde Wright Woodruff:** 15 (Brittle Prickly Pear flower), 24 (Whipple Fishhook Cactus-both) **Rick and Nora Bowers:** all other images

10 9 8 7 6 5 4 3 2 1
Cover and book design by Lora Westberg
Edited by Sandy Livoti
Published by Adventure Publications

This quick guide to cacti of the Southwest is designed to introduce the curious nature seeker to 132 species of cacti. It features full-color images of entire cacti and close-ups of their vivid flowers.

WHAT ARE CACTI?

Cacti are succulents, drought-tolerant plants that store large quantities of water in their fleshy (succulent) stems or roots. Cacti are members of one succulent family, the Cactaceae. For the purposes of this guide, a cactus is defined as having fleshy, leafless stems with waxy, water-retaining skin, and prickly spines emerging in clusters from specialized areas in the skin called areoles. Food production (photosynthesis) in cacti is mainly accomplished in the stems by enlarged green cells that also retain water. Spines provide shade for the stems, reducing water evaporation and form a barrier that defends the plant from being eaten by animals. Cactus flowers are usually handsome, with many similar-looking petals and petal-like sepals, hundreds of pollen-bearing male flower parts (stamens) and several sticky female flower parts (stigmas).

CACTUS BASICS

It's easier to identify cacti and discuss them when you know the names of their different parts. The following illustration points out the basic parts of various cacti. Note: These are for informational purposes only and should not be confused with any specific cactus species.

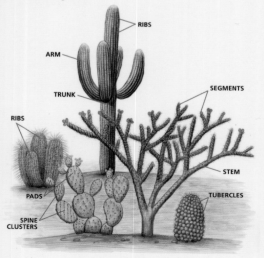

In this guide, cacti are organized in familiar groups (saguaro, prickly pear, etc.), and these groups appear on the tabs to the right. When you've found a cactus you want to identify, first analyze its overall stem shape and compare it with the icons and text description below. After you've identified the appropriate cacti grouping, turn to that tab and examine the photographs, range maps and descriptions to identify your find. Note: Within each grouping, the cacti are loosely organized by size from largest to smallest.

Also keep in mind that many cactus species are protected and collecting or disturbing cacti is illegal without proper licenses or permits.

SAGUARO (COLUMNAR CACTI)

 The largest cacti have tall columns and can be as big as telephone poles or resemble organ pipes. These cacti have ribbed ridges and grooves. Large white or pink-tinged flowers open at night.

CHOLLA AND PRICKLY PEAR

 Cholla are upright and shrubby or tree-like cacti, with slender cylindrical jointed stems that are usually very spiny.

 Club cholla have spiny, club-shaped stems that form dense low-growing mats that hug the ground.

 Prickly pear have flat, paddle-shaped stems; they grow upright or sprawled out.

BARREL AND HEDGEHOG

 Barrel cacti have thick, barrel-shaped stems that can be up to 10 feet tall. Their stem surfaces are ribbed and lined with stout spine clusters.

 Hedgehog cacti have slim stems with vertical folds of ridges and grooves (called ribs) and often grow in clusters. Their flowers, which range significantly in size, bloom just below the tips or along the sides of the stems, emerging through the skin above a mature spine cluster. Their fruit is spiny.

How to Use This Guide

PINEAPPLE AND BEEHIVE

Pineapple cacti are short, pineapple-shaped plants, usually with a single stem with tubercles arranged on vertical ribs rather than in spirals. Blossoms are short, stiff, funnel-shaped and appear in dense tufts at the tip of stems. Their fruit is fleshy and scaly, drying when ripe in most species.

Beehive cacti have globe-shaped stems with a flat top. Cone-shaped bumps (tubercles) on the skin appear in spirals. Each tubercle has a groove on the upper side and a cluster of spines growing from the tip. Beehive cacti often grow as one stem, but some species appear in large clusters or mounds.

FISHHOOK AND PINCUSHION

Fishhook cacti have stout and formidable-looking spines with one or more spines hooked. Well-defined rows of tubercles or prominent ribs twist around a single stem, or clumps of stems. Most have tubercles that are grooved on their upper surfaces. These grooves contain nectar-producing glands and are packed with wool. Flowers sprout from the tips of the stems. Spineless fruit either dries out when mature or remains only slightly fleshy.

Pincushion cacti have short, round stems that usually grow in clusters. Firm conical bumps (tubercles) spiral around the stems. The tubercles are tipped with a cluster of fine spines. Flowers appear in a ring at the top edges of the stems. Pincushion fruit lacks hair, scales or spines.

SMALL SPINELESS

Small spineless cacti lack spines and have smooth or fissured skin. Often rare, these grow low to the ground (withdrawing to below ground level during drought) and are inconspicuous, which helps protect them from being eaten. Their flowers are large in proportion to their stems and sprout from the center of the tops of the stems. Their small fleshy fruit is dry when mature.

Saguaro
10–30' • *Carnegiea gigantea*

largest cactus in U.S.; up to 30 arms, weighs
several tons; Arizona's state flower;
attracts nectar-
feeding bats and
Elf Owls; in Saguaro
National Park

LATE APR–EARLY J

Senita
10–20' • *Lophocereus schottii*

up to 100 hexagonal stems branch at the
ground, beard-like spines at the top;
ants eat nectar by the
spines and protect
the plant from
other insects

APR–S

Barbed Wire Cactus
6–23' • *Acanthocereus tetragonus*

in the frost-free southern parts of Texas and
Florida; spiny, fast-growing stems
are cultivated for use
as barbed fences to
contain livestock

JUL–S

Organ Pipe Cactus
9–20' • *Stenocereus thurberi*

organ pipe-like tall columns; flowers open
after sunset, pollinated by
nectar-feeding bats;
Organ Pipe Cactus
National Monument is
named for it

APR–J

Golden Cereus
2–3' • *Bergerocactus emoryi*

golden-spined slender columns; from
Baja California to San Diego; easily
seen in Cabrillo
National Monument
on Point Loma
Peninsula

MAY–J

Jumping Cholla
6–15' • *Cylindropuntia fulgida*

densely spiny segments detach so readily it
seems to "jump" out to touch you;
grape-like clusters of
fruit stay on for years;
blooms in late afternoon

APR–S

Cholla

Staghorn Cholla
6–12' • *Cylindropuntia versicolor*

slim, antler-like branches; named versicolor
for flowers in rich colors of yellow,
gold, coppery orange,
red, magenta or
purple, all with
yellow centers

APR–JUN

Cane Cholla
3–10' • *Cylindropuntia spinosior*

often grows out in the open; bumpy yellow
fruit stays on all winter; long,
dead branches dry to
hollow canes,
sometimes used as
walking sticks

APR–JUN

Tree Cholla
3–10' • *Cylindropuntia imbricata*

skin has bumps that secrete sweet droplets
on which ants feed; in return, the
ants patrol the cactus
to stop other insects
from eating the stems

MAY–JUN

Buckhorn Cholla
3–10' • *Cylindropuntia acanthocarpa*

large flowers in a variety of bright colors;
American Indians of the desert
Southwest traditionally
steamed and ate
unopened flower buds

APR–MAY

Arizona Pencil Cholla
2–10' • *Cylindropuntia arbuscula*

dense, smooth, pencil-thin stems; branches
form impenetrable thickets; fruit is
mostly infertile, so new
plants start from
broken branches

APR–JUN

Whipple Cholla
4–7' • *Cylindropuntia whipplei*

tree-like with a short trunk, or a creeping mat
of green-to-purple stem segments;
cold tolerant, growing
on high mesas;
favorite food of
the Pronghorn

JUN–JUL

Coastal Cholla
2–8' • *Cylindropuntia prolifera*

upright with stout stems, deep pink flowers and many fruits; on coastal bluffs and sage flats, hills of southwestern California and Channel Islands

APR–JU

California Cholla
1–8' • *Cylindropuntia californica*

two varieties: one snaking and sprawling, one straight and upward; bluffs, chaparral, oak woods; usually less spiny than Gander Cholla

APR–JU

Desert Night-blooming Cereus
2–6½' • *Peniocereus greggii*

dead-looking, stick-like stems; grows under mesquite and ironwood trees; fragrant flowers open for 1 night; nearby cereus bloom simultaneously

MAY–JU

Diamond-plated Pencil Cholla
2–6½' • *Cylindropuntia ramosissima*

shrubby with a diamond-shaped pattern on thin branches; one of the most heat and drought-tolerant chollas; blooms noon to 2 p.m.

MAY–JU

Desert Christmas Cholla
2–6' • *Cylindropuntia leptocaulis*

most widespread and the slimmest stems of any cholla; fruit ripens to red and stays on plant through winter; flowers from 4 p.m. until after dark

MAR–AUG & OC

Klein Pencil Cholla
1½–6' • *Cylindropuntia kleiniae*

upright, scraggly clumps of thin branches, sparsely spined; Chihuahuan and Sonoran Deserts; orange or brown fruit; hybridizes with other slender cholla

MAY–JU

Golden Cholla
3–4' • *Cylindropuntia echinocarpa*

bushy with a squat trunk and short,
branching, jointed stems; dense
spines vary in length,
covering stems in
pale yellow or silver

MAR–MAY

Wolf Cholla
1½–5' • *Cylindropuntia wolfii*

upright with many branches of stout spiny
stems; the earliest blooming cholla,
flower is deep orange
red; in Anza-Borrego
Desert State Park

MAR–MAY

Gander Cholla
1½–5' • *Cylindropuntia ganderi*

upright and graceful, with slender, densely
spiny branches; bur-like spiny fruit;
a very common cholla
in Anza-Borrego
Desert State Park

MAR–MAY

Teddy Bear Cholla
1–5' • *Cylindropuntia bigelovii*

compact with pale spines so dense, the
plant looks cute and fuzzy; stem
segments drop readily;
pack rats gather the
stems to roof their nests

MAR–JUN & SEP AFTER SUMMER RAINS

Chuckwalla Cholla
½–3¾' • *Cylindropuntia chuckwallensis*

newly described cactus in the Eagle Mountains of Joshua Tree National Park;
flowers mainly orange,
but also yellow or dark
reddish purple

APR–MAY

Thistle Cholla
8–34" • *Cylindropuntia davisii*

scattered and uncommon; usually grows as
a single plant; looks like a big clump
of dried grass from a
distance; waxy-looking,
greenish yellow flowers

JUN–JUL

Icicle Cholla
12–24" • *Cylindropuntia tunicata*

formidable-looking; translucent spines
glow as though lit from within
when backlit with low
light, giving them an
ice-coated appearance

MAY–JU

Devil Club Cholla
3–12" • *Grusonia emoryi*

sparsely spiny green stems; yellow-tipped,
tan or reddish brown spines; deserts
in Texas, New Mexico
and Arizona; makes
spiny spreading mats

APR–JU

Parish Club Cholla
2–8" • *Grusonia parishii*

club-shaped, densely spiny stems; yellow
flowers tipped in pink; Sonoran and
Mojave Deserts up to
5,000 feet; in California,
Arizona and Nevada

MAY–J

Club Cholla
1–6" • *Grusonia clavata*

flattened, dagger-like white spines on
low-growing stems; in grasslands
open pinyon-juniper
woods; New Mexico
only; up to 8,000 feet

MAY–JU

Clumped Dog Cholla
1–6" • *Grusonia aggeria*

short, spreading, mounded mats; restricted
to Big Bend area in western Texas
within 20 miles of the
Rio Grande; segments
cling tightly to stems

LATE MAR–A

Schott Club Cholla
3–3½" • *Grusonia schottii*

branches near the ground and forms
creeping mats up to 17' wide; pads
are club-shaped; the
most common club
cholla in Texas

MAY–EARLY J

Sagebrush Club Cholla
1–4" • *Grusonia pulchella*

dies back to tuberous root; beautiful flowers in spring; Great Basin and Mojave Deserts in California, Nevada, Utah

Barberry Fig
10–20' • *Opuntia ficus-indica*

fast-growing and tree-like with a spineless trunk; grown worldwide for its smooth, glossy pads, which can be boiled, pickled or put in salads

APR–EARLY JUN

Pancake Prickly Pear
6½–8' • *Opuntia chlorotica*

Y-shaped with a spiny, knobby trunk and flat, yellowish green pads; on outcrops, ledges, canyons; tolerant of fire; pads toxic to most animals

APR–MAY

Chaparral Prickly Pear
3–10' • *Opuntia oricola*

large and tree-like with one or more trunks; round, thick pads have short, curved yellow spines; in sage scrub, chaparral within 25 miles of the coast

MAY

Texas Prickly Pear
3–10' • *Opuntia engelmannii* var. *lindheimeri*

most abundant and conspicuous in Texas; yellow-spined type grows east of the Pecos River; yellow flowers, also orange, pink or red in south Texas

MID-APR–MAY

Engelmann Prickly Pear
3–10' • *Opuntia engelmannii*

short-trunked with large pads and stubby white spines; dark red pulp of fruit is used to make juices, jelly and even wine!

APR–MAY

Chisos Mountain Prickly Pear
1–3' • *Opuntia chisosensis*

only in the Chisos Mountains in Big Bend National Park; has smaller fruit than other prickly pears in the Chisos Mountains, turns beet red when ripe

MAY–EARLY JU

Santa Rita Prickly Pear
4–7' • *Opuntia santa-rita*

shrubby or tree-like with a short trunk; mostly spineless, bluish green pads turn purple when stressed by drought or cold; often cultivated

APR–EARLY JU

Spinyfruit Prickly Pear
3–5' • *Opuntia spinosibacca*

dotted with rust and white spines; a naturally occurring hybrid and fruit is usually sterile; only on limestone slopes in Big Bend National Park

APR–MA

Blind Prickly Pear
2–6' • *Opuntia rufida*

velvety covering of tiny soft hairs on skin of pads; russet tufts of hair-like spines can cause blindness if they get in the eyes of grazing cattle

APR–MA

Rio Grande Prickly Pear
2–5' • *Opuntia aureispina*

upright, very spiny trunk; bluish green pads with twisted, bright gold spines 2–6" long; only in Big Bend area of Texas along the Rio Grande

MA

Chenille Prickly Pear
2–4' • *Opuntia aciculata*

fuzzy oval pads have rings of hair-like reddish brown spines; yellow or red blossoms; widely cultivated in the U.S., Europe and Australia

APR–MA

Marblefruit Prickly Pear
20–40" • *Opuntia strigil*

densely compact with dark-spotted, evenly spiny pads; marble-sized fruit is the smallest of any prickly pear; found mostly in two Texas counties

EARLY APR–JUN

Big Bend Prickly Pear
12–40" • *Opuntia azurea*

green, reddish purple or lavender pads with very long, flexible spines on the upper part; prickly pears are an important human food in Mexico

MAR–JUN

Border Prickly Pear
20–40" • *Opuntia atrispina*

sprawling with two-toned, reddish brown and yellow spines on upper part of pads; blooms early in spring; grows close to border with Mexico

APR, PERHAPS MAY

Coastal Prickly Pear
1–3' • *Opuntia littoralis*

upright, very spiny trunk; bluish green pads with twisted, bright gold spines 2–6" long; found only in chaparral along southern California coast

MAY

Brown-spine Prickly Pear
1–3' • *Opuntia phaeacantha*

sprawling low clumps; pads streaked red or turn red with age; tulip-shaped yellow or salmon flowers; common cactus across the West

APR–JUN

Black-spine Prickly Pear
1–3' • *Opuntia macrocentra*

broad bluish green pads with tinges of purple; turns red in drought and cold; longest spines of any prickly pear; yellow and red flowers

APR–JUN

Grizzly Bear Prickly Pear
8–24" • *Opuntia polyacantha* var. *erinacea*

small pads with white, flexible spines, making it look grizzled; light yellow flowers tinged bronze; common along Colorado River in Grand Canyon

MAY–JU

Potts Prickly Pear
8–16" • *Opuntia pottsii*

less than 2' wide, with upright or reclining heart- to diamond-shaped pads; spines on upper half of small pads; sometimes all-red flowers

MAY–JU

Western Prickly Pear
6–14" • *Opuntia macrorhiza*

clump-forming small cactus with flattened bluish green pads; one of the most widespread cacti in the west and Midwest

APR–JU

Beavertail Prickly Pear
3–16" • *Opuntia basilaris*

trunkless, spreading clumps; spineless, bluish green pads are shaped like a beaver tail; rows of hairy brown tufts; pads turn purple if stressed

FEB–MA

Pinkava Prickly Pear
4–10" • *Opuntia pinkavae*

small shrub with long straight spines, pink flowers, dry fruit; only in northern Arizona and southern Utah; dry grasslands at 4,000–5,200 feet

MAY–JU

Plains Prickly Pear
3–6" • *Opuntia polyacantha*

spreading mats of paddle-shaped, spiny, segmented stems; cold tolerant and hardy; in western grasslands and pinyon pine/juniper woodlands

JU

Brittle Prickly Pear

1–4" • *Opuntia fragilis*

dense mats of potato-shaped pads; pads detach and take root; rarely blooms; grows farther north than any other cactus; survives temps to -50 °F

APR–JUN

Fishhook Barrel

8" up to 10' • *Ferocactus wislizeni*

stout cactus has bristle-like radial spines with dark tips; large, hooked central spine was once used to catch fish; orange, yellow or red flowers

JUL–OCT

Compass Barrel

18" up to 8' • *Ferocactus cylindraceus*

only barrel cactus in most of its range; interlocking, shady mesh of long spines; lives in drier habitats than other barrel cacti

MAY–JUN

Emory Barrel

12–36" • *Ferocactus emoryi*

round or cylindrical stems with a flat top; taller plants lean southwest; stout, rigid spines on about 30 ribs; cup-like red flowers ring the top

JUL–SEP

Turk's Head Barrel

4–24" • *Ferocactus hamatacanthus*

very spiny and stout; hooked or curved central spines; reddish brown or straw-colored spines hide deeply notched skin above spine clusters

JUN–AUG

Many-headed Barrel

6–16" • *Echinocactus polycephalus*

2–50 stems; no other barrel forms as many stems; red spines glow when wet; dense white hairs on fruit; in Grand Canyon National Park

MAY–JUN

BARREL

Coast Barrel Cactus
4–14" • *Ferocactus viridescens*

main central spine is stout, rigid and points down; along southern coastal California at 30–100 feet; only in San Diego County in the U.S.

MAY–JUL

Eagle's Claw Cactus
2–12" • *Echinocactus horizonthalonius*

bluish gray stem topped with cream-colored wool; 8 broad ribs lined with stout spines; 3 lower spines curve down, like eagle claws

JUN–SEP

Horse Crippler
4–8" • *Echinocactus texensis*

dome-shaped with narrow vertical ribs lined with claw-like spines; sharp central spine is tough enough to puncture a horse's hoof

MAR–MAY

HEDGEHOG

Dahlia Hedgehog
12–24" • *Echinocereus poselgeri*

climbing or sprawling; elongated slim stems have woody cores, providing support; densely interwoven spines press against the stem

MAR–APR

Berlandier Hedgehog
8–25" • *Echinocereus berlandieri*

elongated, freely branching, reclining stems; rare in the wild, mainly in Texas subtropical thorn scrub; flowers have dark pink throats

MAY–JUN

Ladyfinger Hedgehog
4–24" • *Echinocereus pentalophus*

green, red or purple nearly square stems sprawl partly on the ground, ends curve upward; sparse spines; flowers have white or yellow throats

MAR–APR

Nicholas Hedgehog
8–18" • *Echinocereus nicholii*

very spiny yellow clumps of 16–30 stems; spines glow when backlit; tolerates cold poorly; common in Organ Pipe Cactus National Monument

MAR–APR

Pitaya
8–16" • *Echinocereus enneacanthus*

flabby, often sprawling, yellowish green stems; magenta flowers on the sides of stems very near the tips; closely resembles Strawberry Hedgehog

APR–MAY

Engelmann Hedgehog
5½–18" • *Echinocereus engelmannii*

clumps up to 3½' wide; curved or twisted central spines of multiple colors; longest spine is white; pollinated by bees, flowers close at night

MAR–APR

Pink-flowered Hedgehog
4–18" • *Echinocereus fasciculatus*

open clumps of 5–30 shaggy stems; spines straight; 1 much longer dark central spine in the clusters by the top of stem; pink to magenta flowers

MAR–APR

Scarlet Hedgehog/King-cup Hedgehog
4–18" • *Echinocereus coccineus/Echinocereus triglochidiatus*

mounds have up to 300 stems; flowers do not close at night; King-cup and Scarlet Hedgehogs are look-alikes; pollinated by hummingbirds

MAR–JUN

Strawberry Hedgehog
4–12" • *Echinocereus stramineus*

shaggy mounds of 20–500 stems resemble stacks of straw; showy flowers stay open all day; large fruit is juicy, red and tastes like strawberry

LATE MAR–MAY

Green-flowered Hedgehog
3–12" • *Echinocereus viridiflorus*

small-sized and variable; small green, rust, peach, yellow or brown flowers; the most cold-hardy form has yellow-green flowers and grows further north

MAR–JUN

Arizona Rainbow Hedgehog
3–12" • *Echinocereus rigidissimus*

stout stem covered with colored bands formed by pink and white spines; lacks central spines; stem is not prickly but flower buds are very spiny

MAY–JUL

Texas Rainbow Hedgehog
4½–9" • *Echinocereus dasyacanthus*

subtle horizontal bands of alternating colors on stem, each indicating a year's growth; brilliant yellow flowers top the stems

MAR–MAY

Chisos Mountain Hedgehog
5–8" • *Echinocereus chisoensis*

few conical stems with flowers on woolly, spiny stalks; rare and endangered, growing only in a small area of Big Bend National Park

MID-MAR – MID-APR

Bonker Hedgehog
5–8" • *Echinocereus bonkerae*

loose clumps of 5–15 stems; green skin with short spines; magenta-to-dark purple flowers; fruit tastes like strawberry; only found in Arizona

APR

Mexican Rainbow Hedgehog
3–8" • *Echinocereus pectinatus*

usually a single, rounded, smooth-looking stem; white spines, lack of reddish banding separate it from Texas Rainbow; sparsely distributed within range

MAR–MAY

Fendler Hedgehog
3–7" • *Echinocereus fendleri*

sparse spines; often grown for its blooms;
wide-ranging, growing at
higher elevations;
edible sweet fruit

APR–MAY

Lace Hedgehog
3–6" • *Echinocereus reichenbachii*

dark green stem usually obscured by
interlacing stiff radial spines that
look like rows of twin
combs; flame-shaped
pink to magenta flower

APR–MAY

Johnson Pineapple Cactus
4–10" • *Echinomastus johnsonii*

size and shape of a pineapple, covered in
red spines; mostly in Arizona; also
in Nevada, Utah and
California near Death
Valley National Park

MAR–MAY

Santa Cruz Beehive Cactus
4–10" • *Coryphantha recurvata*

mounds of rounded stems can be 36"
wide; central spines curve down;
flowers form a golden
wreath; sometimes
illegally collected

JUN–JUL

Cushion Foxtail Cactus
2–10½" • *Coryphantha alversonii*

dense spines with reddish black tips resemble a fox's tail; two layers of skin
protect from drought;
easily seen in Joshua
Tree National Park

MAY–JUN

Needle-spine Pineapple Cactus
3–9" • *Echinomastus erectocentrus*

pineapple-shaped; bumpy, narrow vertical
ribs; upward-pointing reddish
central spines have
dark tips; pollinated by
native wild bees

MAR–APR

Sneed Beehive Cactus
1–10½" • *Coryphantha sneedii*

white, variable clumps of up to 250 upright rigid stems; wagon wheel-like radiating central spines; several flowers on flat-topped stems

MAR–JUN

Big-needle Beehive Cactus
2–9" • *Coryphantha macromeris*

low-growing mounds with many stems; unusually large bumps tipped with long, untidy spines; blooms 4–6 times in summer after rains

MAY–SEP

Warnock Pineapple Cactus
1½–8" • *Echinomastus warnockii*

whitish green stem with 13 low ribs arranged in spirals; bluish gray spines; 6 species occur in the *Echinomastus* genus in the Southwest

FEB–MAR

Woven-spine Pineapple Cactus
2–7" • *Echinomastus intertextus*

inward-curving spines pressed against the stem; often hidden by grasses in volcanic rocks; coconut-scented pale blooms

FEB–APR

Common Beehive Cactus
1–8" • *Coryphantha vivipara*

solitary or clumped with bumps in spiraling rows; abundant; range covers half of US and parts of Canada; cold-hardy to -40 °F

APR–AUG

Cob Beehive Cactus
2–7" • *Coryphantha tuberculosa*

irregular clumps of various-sized stems; spineless tubercles at the base of older stems look like corncobs; blooms late afternoon and evening

APR–AUG

Robust-spine Beehive Cactus
2–6" • *Coryphantha robustispina*

looks like a tiny barrel cactus with stout spines on pineapple-shaped bumps; flowers for 1 day, 5 days after a rain; western form endangered

APR–SEP

Chihuahuan Beehive Cactus
2–6" • *Neolloydia conoidea*

cylindrical with straight, needle-like spines; cone-shaped bumps spiral in rows around stems; much white wool atop stems

MAINLY MAY–JUN

Mojave Spinystar
1½–6" • *Coryphantha chlorantha*

so similar to Common Beehive Cactus only an expert can distinguish except when blooming; dull orange blooms dry to yellowish green

APR–JUN

Sea Urchin Beehive Cactus
1–6" • *Coryphantha echinus*

1–50 round stems of various ages colored gray or yellowish tan by overlapped stout spines; blooms open at noon for 2–4 hours and for 1 day only

APR–JUL

Lloyd Pineapple Cactus
1–4¾" • *Echinomastus mariposensis*

about the size of a tennis ball and always 1 stem; grows only on limestone, preferring a rockier habitat than any other pineapple cactus

LATE WINTER–EARLY SPRING

Desert Beehive Cactus
1¾–4" • *Coryphantha dasyacantha*

shaggy-spined; *Coryphantha*, derived from Greek for "summit flower," refers to the blooms atop the stems; dry flower tufts remain on ripe fruit

MAR–JUL

Grooved Beehive Cactus
1½–3" • *Coryphantha sulcata*

many soft bumps tipped with short white
wool and stout spines; *sulcata*, Latin
for "furrow," refers to
the groove on the
upper surface of bumps

APR–MAY

Whiskerbush Beehive Cactus
½–3½" • *Coryphantha ramillosa*

dark green stem with conspicuous, conical
bumps; bumps tipped with shaggy
spines and have a
groove on upper
surface from tip to base

AUG–SEP

Missouri Foxtail Cactus
1–3" • *Coryphantha missouriensis*

multiple dark green stems covered with
prominent, conical bumps tipped
with short white wool;
short spines, widely
spaced; cold-hardy

APR–JUN

Junior Tom Thumb Cactus
1¼–2½" • *Coryphantha robertii*

reddish brown or white stems are bristly
and occur in small groups to
bunches; easily seen
by Lake Amistad in
southern Texas; flowers
brown to green

FEB–MAR

Duncan Beehive Cactus
½–1½" • *Coryphantha duncanii*

bristly spines; grows only deep in cracks in
white limestone rocks; flowers open
only on sunny days;
only found in Big Bend
National Park, nowhere
else worldwide

FEB–MAR

Mojave Fishhook Cactus
4–16" • *Sclerocactus polyancistrus*

red and white spines with large fragrant
flowers; native to Mojave Desert in
California, Nevada; in
Joshua Tree and Death
Valley National Parks

APR–JUN

Smallflower Fishhook Cactus
1¾–18" • *Sclerocactus parviflorus*

most common, more widespread, growing
larger than other *Sclerocactus*; in
pinyon-juniper woods,
grasslands, canyons at
3,000–7,000 feet

APR–MAY

Glory-of-Texas
2–15" • *Thelocactus bicolor*

round or conical cactus; spines bicolored
but not hooked; stunning, large
pink flowers in a tuft
at top of stem;
flowering repeats
with rain

FEB–OCT

Clover Eagle-claw Cactus
1–10" • *Sclerocactus cloverae*

stout spines, bottom spine hooked like an
eagle's claw; in desert grasslands,
desert scrub, pinyon-
juniper woods; only in
New Mexico, Colorado

LATE APR–EARLY JUN

Twisted-rib Cactus
2–8" • *Hamatocactus bicolor*

"Twisted-rib" refers to slender, ridged ribs
that spiral around the stem; thinner
radial spines look like
bright white bow ties
sprinkled on the stems

APR–OCT

Chihuahuan Fishhook Cactus
3–6" • *Glandulicactus uncinatus*

stem has deeply notched ribs made up of
compressed bumps; dome-shaped
nectar glands in woolly
grooves; very long
hooked central spines

MAR–MAY

Scheer Fishhook Cactus
1¾–7" • *Ancistrocactus scheeri*

high, very shaggy stem, looking like a small
haystack; glands secrete a high-
sucrose nectar;
has large fleshy roots

NOV–MAR

FISHHOOK

Short-hook Fishhook Cactus
1¾–5" • *Ancistrocactus brevihamatus*

egg-shaped, interesting cactus with formidable-looking spines; 1 stout, hooked central spine; popularly cultivated in Europe

JAN–MAR

Colorado Hookless Cactus
1–5" • *Sclerocactus glaucus*

bluish gray with curved (not hooked) spines and bright red nectar glands; grows only in small area of western Colorado and eastern Utah

APR–MAY

Mesa Verde Fishhook Cactus
1¼–4⅓" • *Sclerocactus mesae-verdae*

unlike other *Sclerocactus*, usually no central spines and has yellow flowers; near Mesa Verde National Park at 4,000–5,000 feet; rare, endangered

LATE APR–EARLY MAY

Whipple Fishhook Cactus
1½–2¾" • *Sclerocactus whipplei*

shaggy, usually single stem; rows of bumps with hooked spines; topmost central spines shaped like daggers; grown indoors in Europe

LATE APR–MAY

PINCUSHION

California Fishhook Pincushion
2–12" • *Mammillaria dioica*

common in coastal scrub near San Diego, also inland; fruit tastes like strawberry crossed with kiwi; usually only *Mammillaria* in its range

MAR–MAY

Arizona Fishhook Pincushion
3–6" • *Mammillaria grahamii*

stiff, rounded stems resembling gray pincushions stuck with hooked pins; conspicuous when flowers bloom about a week after heavy rain

APR–SEP

Rattail Pincushion

2½–6" • *Mammillaria pottsii*

slim cylindrical stems branch from their bases; bluish-purple tipped spines point upward; small rusty or red flowers pollinated by little native bees

FEB–MAR

Corkyseed Fishhook Pincushion

2–6" • *Mammillaria tetrancistra*

dense clumps of 1–8 soft stems; named for cork-like appendages on tiny black seeds; abundant in the Sonoran and Mojave Deserts

APR–JUL

Mountain Ball Cactus

1-6" • *Pediocactus simpsonii*

cold-hardy, up to 11,800 feet in Rocky Mountains, higher than other cacti; widespread but not common; shape and number of spines vary

APR–JUL

Greenflower Pincushion

2–4" • *Mammillaria viridiflora*

cream, pale greenish white or rose-pink flowers; in grasslands, chaparral and woodlands on gravelly slopes; hooked central spine is dark red

SPRING

Thornber Fishhook Pincushion

2–4" • *Mammillaria thornberi*

dense clumps of bumpy stems; hooked central spines; rings of star-shaped pink flowers; much like the more common Arizona Fishhook

APR–MAY, JUL–AUG

Wright Pincushion

1½–4" • *Mammillaria wrightii*

large pink to magenta flowers bloom after summer rains; green to dull purple globular fruit; on slopes in grasslands, pinyon-juniper woods

JUL–AUG

Pincushion

MacDougal Pincushion
1–3" • *Mammillaria macdougalii*

disk-shaped cactus with depressed top
wreathed with brown-striped
yellow flowers; also
called Cream
Pincushion due to
milky sap

APR–MAY

Brady Pincushion
1–2½" • *Pediocactus bradyi*

also called Marble Canyon Pincushion; a
rare, endangered cactus in Grand
Canyon National Park,
and the Navajo Nation
among limestone chips

LATE MAR–MID-APR

Longmamma Pincushion
1½–2" • *Mammillaria sphaerica*

lumpy, pale green mounds; 10–30 knobby
stems with sparse, thin spines;
fragrant large flowers;
ripe fruit smells sweet,
with an apple-like flavor

JUL–AUG

Navajo Pincushion
¾–2½" • *Pediocactus peeblesianus*

flexible spongy spines are stout and
curved; endangered; in the Grand
Canyon near the
Colorado and Little
Colorado Rivers;
belowground in drought

SPRING

Little Pincushion
1–2" • *Mammillaria meiacantha*

broad, flat, green stem covered with closely
spaced, prominent conical green
bumps (tubercles)
with few spines; can
grow to 6–12" wide

MAR–MAY

Texas Pincushion
½–2" • *Mammillaria prolifera*

dense mounds of egg-shaped, fuzzy stems
with soft, curly, hair-like spines;
commonly cultivated,
easy to grow indoors;
has bright red fruit

MAR

Button Cactus

½–2" • *Epithelantha micromeris*

button-sized; can bloom when the size of a penny; has the smallest flowers of all cacti; Tarahumara Indians ingest this cactus for strength

FEB–APR

Ping Pong Ball Cactus

¾–1¼" • *Epithelantha bokei*

densely covered with layers of highly reflective, hair-like spines that provide shade for stem; tolerates heat up to 140 °F

MAY–JUN

Golfball Pincushion

½–1½" • *Mammillaria lasiacantha*

miniature round cactus with densely overlapping white spines; widely distributed in Texas and New Mexico; one of the earliest to bloom

FEB–MAR

Heyder Pincushion

¼–1" • *Mammillaria heyderi*

disk-shaped with flat top ringed by pink-striped cream blossoms; its milky white sap is sold as a folk remedy in Mexico; cold-hardy; easy to grow

MAR–APR

Star Cactus

1–2½" • *Astrophytum asterias*

8 broad, pie-shaped ribs topped with gray woolly tufts and separated by grooves dotted with white; also called Sand Dollar Cactus

MAR–MAY

Living Rock Cactus

ground level–¾" • *Ariocarpus fissuratus*

spineless, multiple-pointed, leathery star; sinks into ground during dry weather; contains substances once used in spiritual ceremonies

SEP–NOV

Adventure Quick Guides

Only Southwest Cacti
Organized by group for
quick and easy identification

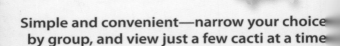

Simple and convenient—narrow your choice by group, and view just a few cacti at a time

- Pocket-sized format—easier than laminated foldouts
- Professional photos showing key markings
- Cactus size and flowering details for quick comparison and identification
- Easy-to-use information for even casual observers
- Based on the field guides by Nora and Rick Bowers

Collect all the Adventure Quick Guides for the Southwest

ISBN 978-1-59193-582-7

$9.95

adventure
PUBLICATIONS
Adventure Publications
820 Cleveland Street South
Cambridge, Minnesota 55008
(800) 678-7006
www.adventurepublications.net
NATURE/CACTI/SOUTHWEST

9 781591 935827